D.I.Y. GUITAR REPAIR

T0057732

Cover design: Fresh Lemon
Interior design and layout: The Bookmakers, Inc.
Interior photography and illustrations by Pieter J. Fillet

This book Copyright © 1984 by Amsco Publications,
A Division of Music Sales Corporation, New York

Order No. AM 38530
ISBN-13: 978-0-8256-3690-5

Printed in the United States of America.

EXCLUSIVELY DISTRIBUTED BY

HAL•LEONARD®

Acknowledgements

I would like to thank the following for their help and guidance in producing this book: Elizabeth Phillips for modeling in some of the pictures, her sister Ellen for helping me make some of the pictures, Garrett A. Randolph for letting me set up and photograph his new guitar that he is shown doing a fret job on, Jim Sheraden for helping me with my English, Mike Lennon at The Apprentice Shop who taught me the basics of guitar repair, Lois Phillips for some wonderful country dinners, all the typing and encouragement, Nashville Music Company and Hewley's Music Store for their cooperation and special thanks to Dr. Carl Phillips, who had to put up with all this. . .

Contents

Introduction

The term "set-up," used by a professional guitar repairman, can be re-read to mean "guitar adjustment," which is exactly what a set-up involves . . the re-adjustment of your valued stringed instrument. Since you have already purchased this manual, we can assume you will attempt it by yourself—an enviable stepping stone along your road of becoming more familiar with and receiving more performance from your guitar. The set-up instructions here are, in the author's opinion, all the steps which are feasible and safe as home adjustments by a competent guitar owner.

While steps can be extracted one by one from the set-up to fit the individual adjustments of your instrument, **it is most important that you take the steps in the order shown.** Most of the tools needed will hang on everyone's basement wall or in the tool chest in the back of the car; others will have to be purchased as required. All of the tools in this book should be familiar to everyone and easy to use. The total set-up of an acoustic guitar is usually different and more difficult than the set-up of an electric guitar. This will sometimes require an operation that I do not consider to be a part of maintenance or set-up, but rather an actual repair situation and therefore I will not always describe this in detail. When I do, it is so you will know how the job needs to be done in case you want to take your instrument to a repairman, or if you want to try it yourself anyway.

Also, I will presume that the neck is correctly attached to the body. If that is not the case, your instrument needs a so-called "neck-set" and this is a major repair situation (except for guitars with bolt on necks, for instance electric Fender guitars) which I will not deal with in this book.

The last thing I want to mention is that although all the parts are separately treated and the work is done in separate steps, you should always remember that a guitar is an instrument where all the individual parts work together as a whole. So if you change one part you may have to change all other parts. That's why it is so important that you go by the steps in the order shown.

Proper guitar adjustment takes time. But in the end, your patience will be rewarded with a smooth playing guitar and the knowledge that you did it yourself!

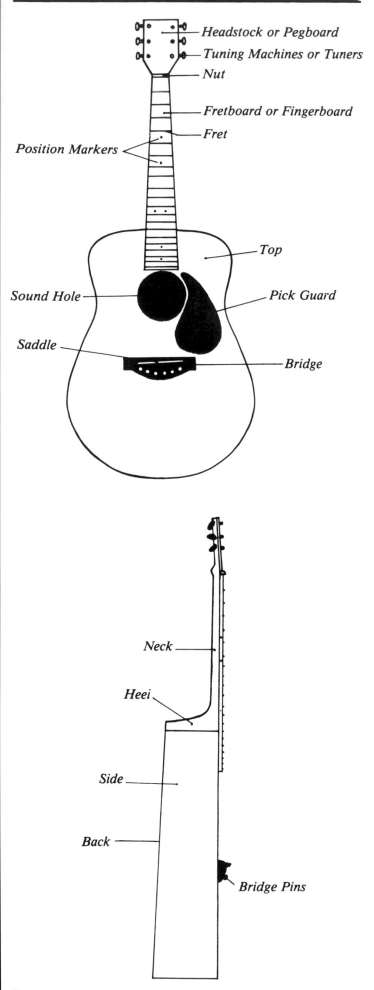

Headstock or Pegboard
Tuning Machines or Tuners
Nut
Fretboard or Fingerboard
Fret
Position Markers
Top
Sound Hole
Pick Guard
Saddle
Bridge
Neck
Heel
Side
Back
Bridge Pins

Figure 1

CHAPTER I

Why a Set-Up?

For your guitar to give its best performance it will have to be "set-up" to your individual standards. You probably need to do this when:

I. You buy a guitar (new or old)

II. You change to a different string gauge

III. You change your music style

IV. After extended use; like a car, your guitar needs a tune-up

I. **When you buy a guitar,** even when it's brand new, most likely your instrument is not set-up properly. Most guitar factories don't seem to bother with it; some have a standard set-up. One reason is that everyone has different ideas about a comfortable set-up. This manual will also give you tips on buying a guitar and it will enlighten you to the possibilities of your instrument and show, for example, that a guitar with strings very high above the fingerboard (a common symptom of a "bad" guitar) is not necessarily an unplayable instrument.

II. Since **different gauges of strings** have different effects on the neck because of differing tensions, some adjustment may be needed.

III. A guitar player with a finger-picking **style** wants an easy to play guitar with strings close to the fretboard, while a bluegrass player or rhythm player needs the strings set up higher so the strings won't rattle.

IV. Because a *guitar is being played and carried around* and very often is exposed to different weather situations (hot/cold, dry/humid) you'll have to set-up your guitar every once in a while. Although you will find that, provided you have a good guitar, this will not very often be the case if you've done a good set-up in the first place.

The following picture gives us the parts of the guitar that will be involved in our set-up. *(Figure 1)*

CHAPTER II

Some Tips on Buying a Guitar

Ideally, one wants to make as few adjustment as possible when purchasing a guitar. Some things to consider are:

Do you need the guitar to be repairable and to what extent? Are spare parts available? Does the guitar's construction (i.e. how its's glued) allow for repair?

Most, if not all, Japanese guitars are glued together with epoxy, polyvinyl, or similar products instead of wood glue. This is a problem if repair is needed because these glues do not soften easily and so cannot be taken apart without great risk.

Condition of the neck

A specific you need to watch out for is the condition of the neck. Check to see if it's warped or not straight. It's best to buy a guitar with an adjustable trussrod, especially if you want to be able to set-up your own guitar. Martin guitars don't have an adjustable trussrod, but are very repairable since the materials used are of solid good quality and all spare parts are readily available. Make sure that the neck is not severely bowed (in the event that you just can't let the guitar go) and that it can be adjusted. *(See Step 5,* **Straightening the Neck)** Do **not** buy a guitar with a warped neck. This means it is twisted over the full length of the wood. See the exaggeration of *Figure 2*. This is almost impossible to repair satisfactorily, if at all.

Figure 2

Check to see if the neck is properly fused to the body. You can use the following methods:

Grab the neck close to the heel with one hand and grab the body of the guitar with the other hand then twist the opposite direction to see if there's any "play" at the joint. If so, the neck is loose and not properly fused to the body. With electric Fenders and other bolt-on neck types, this can usually be easily fixed. However, it is a major repair for acoustic guitars and, at the time of this writing, will cost at least $85.00 to $100.00.

To check the right angle of the neck of an acoustic guitar, you have to check if the neck is in a straight line with the guitar top *(Figures 3a, 3b, 3c)*. You can do this with a straight edge. Loosen the strings so the neck is free of string tension. If you want to be very particular about this, then you have to loosen the tension of the adjustable trussrod, if there is one. *(See Step 5)* You can double-check this by looking down the neck. *(Figure 3d)* Follow the broken line over the top of the fingerboard (the actual board and not the top line of the frets). The line will have to come about 1 mm – 2 mm (0.04 - 0.05 inches) under the top of the bridge. Therefore, distance *a* must be smaller than 2 mm. If the distance is greater than 2 mm, then it is likely that the neck is not properly fixed to the body and will need what is called a "neck-set," provided that the bridge is not too high.

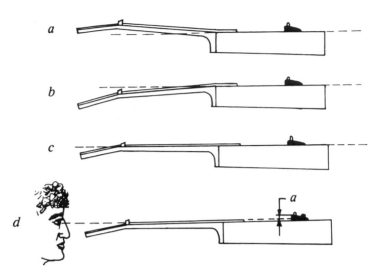

Figure 3

EXCEPTIONS: Guitars with bolt-on necks can easily be helped with a "shim" (small piece of wood, plastic, or cardboard). *(See Figure 61 and Figure 62)* With classical or "Spanish" guitars, the *a* distance is always much greater and a neck-set in the sense of how we know it with flattops will be impossible since they have an integral neck joint (neck and neck block is in one piece).

NOTE: Most electric Gibsons and other electric guitars with glued in necks have a neck with an angle of about 5° backwards. They look somewhat like *Figure 3b*.

The next thing you want to **make sure is that the acoustic guitar has a perfectly straight top.** Sometimes it happens that a guitar for sale has a top slightly swollen behind the bridge. If it is swollen, the chances are good that it is also bent in **front** of the bridge. *(See Figure 4)* The problem can be:

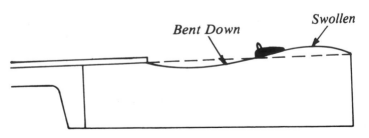

Bent Down *Swollen*

Figure 4

A. One or more braces (the stiffeners under the top) or the bridge plate (plate under bridge on inside of guitar) are loose. If you're examining the guitar in a music store, ask the dealer for a small inspection mirror and check with a little light through the sound hole. *(Figure 5)* Look, via the inspection mirror, at the braces and bridge plate while you press firmly on the top of the guitar and see if the braces move. If so, the swell can be corrected by re-gluing. Although this is a relatively simple and inexpensive repair, it should be done by a professional repairman.

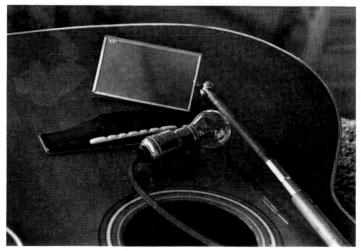

Figure 5

B. If you cannot find loose braces or a loose bridge plate, then the guitar is likely not to be constructed properly and the materials used are not strong and/or thick enough. In that case, DON'T BUY!!

Most Japanese guitars have a polyurathene finish. In a repair situation this is a problem if you want to do a touch-up job, since the new finish won't blend in with the old. In this event, even the most expert touch-up will reveal a "ghost line" at best. You won't have that problem with guitars that have the conventional lacquer finishes. New lacquer will blend invisibly with the old lacquer. Check also all parts that are glued together; make sure that they are!!

One last thing: Acoustic guitars with an oval sound hole will very likely give you problems in case of a number of repairs. I'm talking about any repairs when the repairman has to put his hands through the sound hole. Oval sound holes are just not big enough to do this. In that case the back of the guitar may have to be taken off, making a repair much more expensive.

CHAPTER III

Some Tips Before We Start

To do a good job on your guitar, it is best to secure your guitar from moving while you are working on it. This is, of course, a must when you dress the frets. Other jobs will go so much easier and better when you do. A very good way of doing this is to clamp your guitar neck in a vise. The vise (preferably one you can swivel around) should be fixed in a manner that will allow you to stand behind your guitar while working on it. This can be done by fixing the vise at the corner of a workbench. *(Figure 6)*

Top View

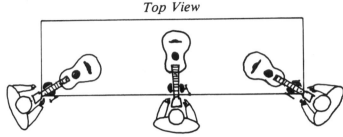

Figure 6

A perfect situation is a "swivel type" vise mounted on a Black & Decker Workmate. *(See Figure 7)* This is portable in case you are "on the road." I had to drill one more hole in the top to be able to mount the vise on the Workmate. The other two holes I needed are already there. I opened up the wooden vise of the Workmate and clamped a piece of wood of the same length and about five inches wide

Figure 7

between them. This gave me a nice table top that is wide enough. On top of this you have to put a scrap piece of carpet or something else that is soft and thick enough to protect your guitar from getting damaged or scratched. I got some sample pieces of carpet, for free, at a carpet store which are just the right size. To protect your neck from getting damaged in the vise, you will have to make some kind of protection. I made one out of two pieces of particle board and a piece of soft leather glued in between with contact cement (as you see in *Figure 8)*. It fits the vise as shown in *Figure 9*. The whole arrangement is shown in *Figure 10*.

Figure 8

Figure 9

Figure 10

When you are working on your guitar and don't really need it clamped up, a good idea is to make a neck rest—a block of wood covered with a soft material (in this case a piece of soft leather) in which you can support the neck. *(See Figure 11)* This will keep your guitar from rocking. Don't forget to put something soft (piece of carpet) under your guitar to keep it from scratching. *(Figure 12)*

Figure 11

Figure 12

The tools you will need are some screwdrivers and/or Phillips screwdrivers and/or Allen wrenches. It all depends on the hardware used on your guitar. Also you will need to make some files if you want to dress frets. In all cases, it will be mentioned and shown at the particular step. When you work with "Krazy Glue," Superglue, or other brands of cyanoacrylate glue, always keep some acetone handy, in case you glue your skin together.

Always read each step completely and make sure that you understand the whole procedure before you start working.

CHAPTER IV

The Set-Up

STEP 1. **Take Off Old Strings**

To do a good set-up, you must put new strings on your guitar. This is illustrated in *Step 8.* Be careful when taking the old strings off. Don't just cut them with a pair of pliers but instead use your tuning pegs to release the tension off them first. Showing your guitar this consideration will prevent your neck from dealing with fast and strong changes in tension.

STEP 2. **Check for Loose Frets**

Often you will hear a "buzz" in your guitar caused by loose frets. Check them all, one by one, by pressing one end of the fret in with your finger and then letting go to see if there is any movement. Since you sometimes have to press quite hard to find out, I suggest you use the point of some pliers or a similar instrument which is not too sharp. Be careful not to damage the fretboard. Do this on both sides of the fret. *(Figure 13)*

STEP 3. **Fix Loose Frets**

To fix loose frets you will have to determine which of the ends are loose. You then place your guitar on its side so that the loose end of the fret is on top. Now press the loose end to the fingerboard with your plier point and let one drop of "Krazy Glue" (or similar type of super glue) fall on the side of the fret so the glue will run down between the fret and board.* Press the fret down until the glue is dry. It shouldn't take long—just a few minutes. *(Figure 14)*

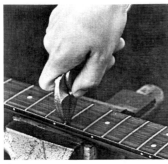
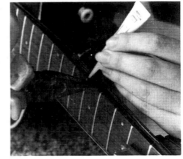

Figure 13 *Figure 14*

Be very careful with the "Krazy Glue." It will glue your skin together in a second. Use acetone to take it off. **NEVER** apply acetone to your guitar, for any reason, since it might damage the finish already there by dissolving it. Excess glue on the side of the fingerboard can be sanded off with very fine (600 grit) sandpaper. Go over all your loose fret ends with this procedure and you will have your

---

*"Krazy Glue" or similar types of super glues are all so-called cyano-acrylate glues. Any of the brands will be fine.

first problem solved. If this system of fixing loose frets does not work for you, then the problem may be more complicated and you may want to visit your guitar repairman.

STEP 4. Check Your Neck

The first thing you will have to do is to check if the neck is warped by looking down the guitar. I mentioned this in the previous chapter entitled "Tips on Buying a Guitar."

If it is warped you have a big problem and you'll have to take it to a professional repairman. He can do the following:

A. Sand or shave down the fingerboards so that the warp "seems" to be gone (frets have to be taken off).

B. Heat the neck and try to bend it back straight. (You're lucky if that works for a while.)

C. Take the fingerboard off and shave the neck until it's straight and then replace the fingerboard (frets don't have to be taken off in this case).

D. Replace the entire neck.

Steps **A** and **C** will not really be the proper repair (it just masks the problem) but can last well. Step **B** would be a proper repair, but usually doesn't last long, if it works at all. Step **D** is usually the best alternative, if you can afford it. It will probably be the cheapest solution in the end, although none of the repairs will be inexpensive.

If your neck is not warped then you can check to see if it's straight. The best way to check this is to take a **straight edge** *(Figure 16)* and lay it lengthwise on top and in the middle of the fingerboard. Be sure that you don't put it on top of the nut or on the saddle, in case you have a very long "straight edge," because then you are not checking the neck. *(Figure 15)* Instead of an expensive "straight edge" you can use an inexpensive **stripper guide** (used for painting) *(Figure 16)* or an eighteen-inch ruler. A ruler does not constitute a straight edge. While it may appear to be straight chances are that it isn't. Another way to make a straight line is with a **string.** First attach a string to the

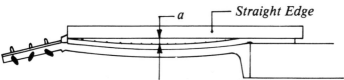

Figure 15

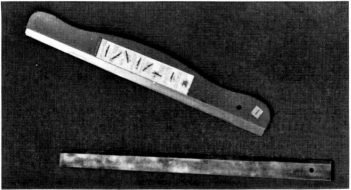

Figure 16

tuner. Press the string down in front of the nut behind the 1st fret with one finger and with the other hand press down behind the last fret of the fingerboard (behind the 12th or 14th fret will usually be all right since this covers the part of the neck that can be adjusted). Make sure you stretch the string tightly so you'll get a straight line. *(Figure 17)*

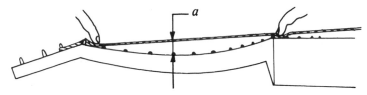

Figure 17

To check if the neck is straight, you can:

a. Find no space at all between the frets and the "straight edge"; all frets should touch the "straight edge." This means the neck is straight. *(Figure 18)*

b. Find a distance "a" (this distance is usually the largest near the 5th and 6th fret) between the "straight edge" and the fretboard. This means the neck has a "hollow" bend. *(Figure 19)*

c. Find a distance "b" between the "straight edge" and the fingerboard at each side. If you can "rock" the "straight edge" the neck has a back bow. *(Figure 20)*

NOTE: If you use the method of checking with the string, then you can only: 1) Find a distance "a" between the string and fingerboard. This means a "hollow" neck. 2) Find the string touching the fingerboard all along the length of the string. This can mean that the neck is straight or (and this is likely) that the neck has a back bow. In that case the flexible string would follow the line of the fingerboard. You can see that this is not a very accurate way to find out.

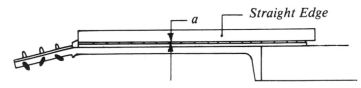

Figure 18

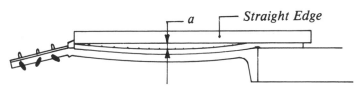

Figure 19

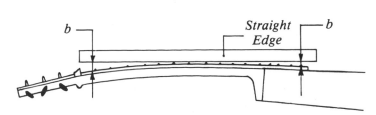

Figure 20

STEP 5. Straightening the Neck

A. Necks with an adjustable trussrod

The trussrod is a steel rod put in the neck for reinforcement. It does not, as a lot of people seem to think, adjust the angle of how the neck is fixed to the guitar body. Trussrods can only straighten the neck between the nut and usually (depending on the system used) the 12th or 14th fret. *(Figure 21)*

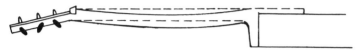

Figure 21

Necks with an adjustable trussrod have a nut screwed on a rod sticking out on one end of the neck. Most often you will find this in the headstock under a little coverplate (for instance Gibson guitars). *(Figures 22a, 22b, and 22c)* Or you

Figure 22a   *Figure 22b*

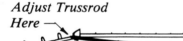

Adjust Trussrod Here ⟵

Figure 22c

may find it on the other end of the neck as is the case with many Fender guitars *(Figures 23a and 23b)* or other "bolt

Figure 23a

Adjust Trussrod Here ⟶

Figure 23b

on'' neck types. This is true also with acoustic guitars (for instance Gallagher). In this case you can reach the nut through the sound hole but it is not an easy thing to do. *(Figures 24a and 24b)* Do not attempt to straighten the neck with your strings tuned to pitch. First take the strings off or at least loosen the strings liberally.

Figure 24a

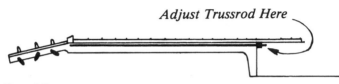

Adjust Trussrod Here

Figure 24b

Straightening out the neck with a trussrod is simple. *(Figure 25)* A neck with a hollow bend is corrected by turning the nut clockwise, using the proper wrench for your guitar, and continuing to compare the new ''arrangement'' with your straight edge. Hopefully you received a wrench with your guitar purchase, otherwise you will have to buy one that fits. There is a variety of wrenches used by the different guitar factories. *(Figure 26)*

Figure 25   Figure 26

I can only say that if you can't buy the right wrench at your music store, you'll have to use your imagination and go to the hardware store and find one that fits or that you can modify. When you have to do that, take your guitar with you to the store so you can try out different types of wrenches.

Be very careful and tighten little by little, not more than a quarter turn at a time and remember to check with your straight edge or with the string method. If a back bow is found in the neck then you will have to loosen up the nut by turning it counterclockwise (to the left). Checking with your straight edge, the neck should come to a straight position. It sometimes doesn't work because the trussrod has accidentally been glued to the wood of the neck. In this case, you can help the neck a little by turning the nut comfortably loose and supporting the neck at both ends. Press with one hand at the middle of the neck. Be careful and don't break anything. *(Figure 27)* Remember the end of the neck at the place of the nut is the weakest spot. You may hear the neck crack. This should be the breaking of the glue that held the trussrod from moving. With an acoustic guitar, if your nut is on the inside, the procedure is more difficult. You may need to use a small inspection mirror and a light *(Figure 5)* to check its position. You must use your own judgment for the rest of the procedure since you have to feel it, because you won't be able to see anything when your hand goes through the sound hole.

Figure 27

B. *Necks without an adjustable trussrod*

To straighten a neck without an adjustable trussrod (example: all "Martin" acoustic guitars and classical guitars, which don't have a trussrod at all) I recommend that you do not do this yourself but get a professional repairman to tackle this problem for you. For the sake of being complete and in order for you to know how it is done, I will explain this operation. It is called a **heatset.**

You will need a few special wooden jigs that you can make from any hardwood (I used maple in this case). Mind the direction of the grain. It must run lengthwise. The first one looks like *Figure 28;* the other one like *Figure 29.* You also need a 250 watt heat lamp with holder, two clamps and some thick leather strips (at least ⅟₁₆ " thick.). When you have a neck with a back bow, work as follows:

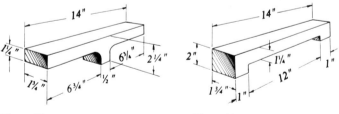

Figure 28   Figure 29

1. Lay the guitar flat on its back. (You have already taken the strings off.)

2. Protect the inlay in the fingerboard (if you have any) with strips of leather. In the same way, protect the binding on the side of the neck, if there is any.

3. Protect the top of the guitar with a piece of cardboard.

4. Place the heat lamp over the middle of the neck (at about the 5th fret from the top). Don't hang the heat lamp too close. Ten inches is usually a good distance. Heat lamps give off infra-red rays so the heat goes through the wood.

Let the lamp heat the neck until you feel its underside getting warm. As a result the wood will be relatively easy to bend back to an accurate shape. This is tricky because you don't want the fingerboard or lacquer to burn up. It should take approximately 15–20 minutes. Never walk away! If you need to leave, disconnect the heat lamp. *(Figure 30)*

Figure 30

5. The neck is now prepared to put jig no. 1 *(Figure 28)* in the center of the bend after you've turned off the heat lamp and taken away the leather strips.

6. Put the clamps on each side of the jig around the neck and tighten these enough so that the neck gets a little "hollow" bend. In other words, go past the point where the neck will be straight. Here is where experience comes in. There is no way I can tell you how much you have to "over bend" because every piece of wood will react differently. It is just a matter of trial and error. *(Figure 31)*

The reason you have to over bend is that, even when the neck has cooled off, the wood tends to want to flex back to the old position and it will just a little. Be careful that the neck is protected from damage by the clamps. A good way is to make some small wood blocks (about 1″ [2½ cm] wide) with the round shape of the neck cut out on one side. Then glue in some leather strips with contact cement. *(Figure 32)*

Figure 31

Figure 32

7. Now you let the neck cool off, at least overnight.

8. When the neck has cooled, take away the clamps; hopefully you have a straight neck. With the neck in the new position, the glue under the fretboard will be dried again, and this will help keep the neck straight. Whether you've over bent the neck too much or not enough will now be apparent. Perhaps you will have to start all over again.

NOTE: If you use a light gauge string and find you have a slightly hollow neck, you may want to leave it since a little relief is needed anyway, *(see Step 9)*. In order to go ahead to "dress your frets" *(Step 7)* you must have a perfectly straight neck.

When the neck has a hollow bow, follow the same steps 1 through 7, with the exception that you now use jig no. 2 *(Figure 29)* and you need only one clamp. This, too, must be over bent a little, and again, this is where experience is helpful. In this case you get the following set-up. *(Figure 33)*

Figure 33

STEP 6. Check for Uneven Frets

Now that the neck is straight, the next event in a set-up is to check for uneven frets. It may be that some stick out higher than others. One reason for uneven frets is that they may be loose. Go back to *Step 2* and *Step 3.* Or you might have worn out frets (especially the first five). Consequently, what we have to do is to make them all even, because it is probably not necessary to replace them yet. *Step 7* will show you how. We often call this dressing, honing, or filing frets. Replacing frets will not be described in this book since it is a major repair.

STEP 7. Dressing, Filing, or Honing Frets

To do a proper job you will need a few special tools, all of which you can easily make. Tools needed:

A. The first tool is a flat mill file about 1″ wide and 8″ or 9″ long. These are available at any hardware store for a few dollars. Lay the file flat and make sure it's straight! Since the file has a sharply tapered end over which a wooden handle would normally fit, we are going to modify it a little. We want to get rid of this sharp point, because it will be in the way. *(Figure 34)*

I don't know all the different ways to tackle this problem but here is one. Put the file in a vise with just the point sticking out. Take a hammer and just knock it off. Watch out! The point will break easily (the material is very hard) and might fly far away and cause some damage. *(Figure 35)* Smooth out the sharp edges of the break *(Figure 36)* on a bench grinder or belt or disc sander *(Figure 37)*. The local machine shop might help you out for free. It will look somewhat like this. *(Figure 38)*

In order to utilize this tool for our needs, it requires a special wooden handle. Take a piece of wood, a little smaller than the file and round off all the edges so that it feels good in your hands. *(Figure 39)* Glue it on the file with epoxy glue. I suggest that you use an epoxy glue that has to dry for at least 10 hours or so, preferably 24 hours, since you want the tool to last after going to all this trouble. A five minute epoxy will work also. When glued together it will look like this. *(Figure 40)*

Figure 34

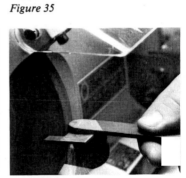

Figure 35

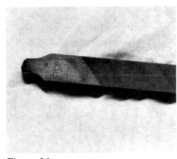

Figure 36

Figure 37

Figure 38

Figure 39

Figure 40

B. The next tool is the small three corner file (about 6″ long). *(Figure 41)* You can use a set of fret files instead which are very nice but are very expensive. All you have to do to modify this three corner file for our purpose is to grind off the sharp corner edges. This works best on a belt sander. When it's finished it looks like this. *(Figure 42)* It will perform a lot better if you put a wooden handle on the file.

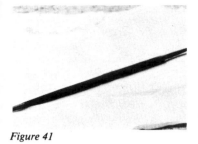

Figure 41   Figure 42

C. You need some 100 grade, 240 grade, and 320 grade sandpaper, or even 600 if you wish.

D. 00 steel wool (very fine)

E. A sharp utility knife blade (only the blade!)

F. A magic marker (black or other dark color) with a thick end.

Now we can start the job, but first the parts of the guitar that can be damaged need to be protected. The sure way to go, especially with lacquered fingerboards, such as Fenders', is to tape the whole fretboard with masking tape leaving the frets exposed. *(Figure 43)* Then (for acoustic guitars) we make a protection plate out of a piece of cardboard shaped like this. *(Figure 44)*

You have to find your own dimensions for the plate because every neck has a slightly different size. This piece goes in between the neck and the bridge. Tape it to the guitar body with masking tape. *(Figure 45)*

1. Clamp your guitar (in a vise) so it won't shift. The easiest and best way is to clamp it so that you can stand behind the headstock.

Figure 43

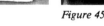

Figure 44   Figure 45

2. Protect the fingerboard with masking tape if it is lacquered and the guitar top with a piece of cardboard, as described before. (Electric guitars: since pick-ups are magnetic, tape them with masking tape so the file shavings won't stick to them.)

3. *Although it is not absolutely necessary,* I like to take off the nut. This is very easy. Take a small piece of wood and tap it with a small hammer while holding it against the nut. *(Figure 46)* **Go Slow! Be Careful!** When it's loose, you tap the wood on the side of the nut and the nut will then slide out of the slot. *(Figure 47)* **(Note:** If you have a zero fret right next to the nut you *must* take this nut off to achieve even fret honing.)

3. Now run your magic marker over the full length of each fret so they are all marked. *(Figure 48)*

5. Take your flat mill file. Stand behind the headstock and lay the file lengthwise on the frets. *(Figure 49)*

6. Now carefully file all the frets with long strokes from the headstock all the way down the end of the fretboard. Use both your hands to control the file, using light but even pressure. Continue to do this until the fret tops shine all the way across. Here is where the marker shows its magic, because you can see where the frets are down by looking at where the color of the magic marker has been filed off. As long as you see a marked spot on the top of a fret, **you must continue filing along the full length of the fretboard. Do not try to work one fret at a time.** *(Figures 49–51)*

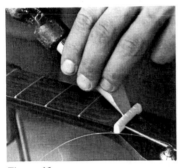

Figure 46

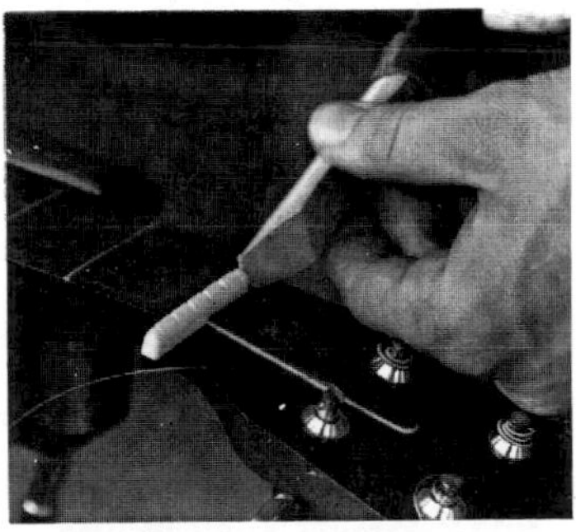

Figure 47

Figure 48

Figure 49

Figure 50

Figure 51

7. Now we'll have to file off the sharp edges of the frets. We can do that with so-called fret files or with our modified three corner file. Stand beside your guitar neck. Then take this file and lightly file off the sharp edges on each side of the fret. Do not touch the top of the frets! Now you can see why the corners of the file had to be smooth, otherwise they would cut into the wood of the fingerboard. *(Figures 52a and 52b)* At the end of the fretboard I find it easier to file one half of the fret, then move over to the other side of the guitar and finish the other half of the fret. *(Figure 53)*

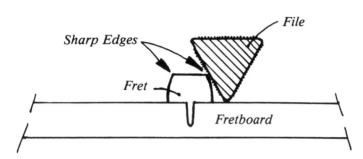

Figure 52a

Figure 52b   Figure 53

8. Remove the protective masking tape from the fingerboard.

9. Now we will take our sharp utility knife blade and hold it in both hands while standing behind the headstock. We will now **scrape off all the marks that you have made with your three corner file.** Also, this is the way to clean up your fingerboard and even out the fingerboard a little where you may have made dips by pressing down the strings. Scrape all the way between the frets. Don't worry, you're not taking off too much and don't be bothered about scraping any inlay. *(Figure 54)* Work the whole neck this way.

10. Now take the utility knife blade in one hand and with one corner of the blade scrape lengthwise along the fret to remove any dirt or wood scrapings. *(Figure 55)*

11. Take one-half sheet of 100 grade sandpaper. Fold it in half and sand over the full length of the fingerboard. Hold the sandpaper down with just your fingertips so that it will nicely shape the edges of the frets. Do this until the file marks are gone. *(Figure 56)*

12. Now take 240 grade sandpaper and do the same thing until the 100 grade marks are gone.

13. Take the 320 grade sandpaper and do the same. If you want it still smoother, repeat with 600 grit sandpaper.

14. Take the steel wool and briskly go over the full length of the neck. This will polish your frets as well as your fingerboard. **Wow!** *(Figure 57)* Finish this off by rubbing on a few drops of lemon oil or vegetable oil.

15. If you have taken the nut off: clean glue and/or bits of wood *(Figure 58)* off the nut using a utility knife or some fine sandpaper and glue it back in place with a few drops of "Krazy Glue." *(Figure 59)* If you wish, you can also polish the nut with some steel wool.

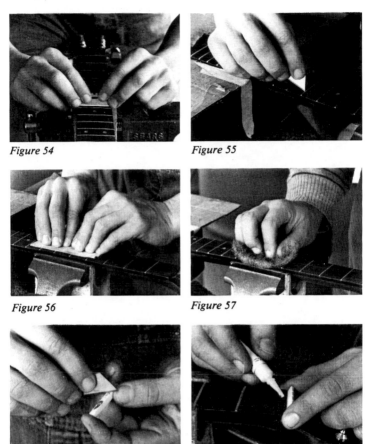

Figure 54

Figure 55

Figure 56

Figure 57

Figure 58

Figure 59

16. If you have a bolt-on type neck and you've taken it off, then you'll have to put it back on the body again. *(Figure 60)* Adjust, if necessary, the neck angle. You can adjust your neck angle by putting shims (small pieces of wood) under the neck *(Figures 61 and 62)* until you get your neck in a straight line with the body as in Figure 60. Some Fender guitar necks are bolted to the body with three screws. With these necks you'll find a little hole with an

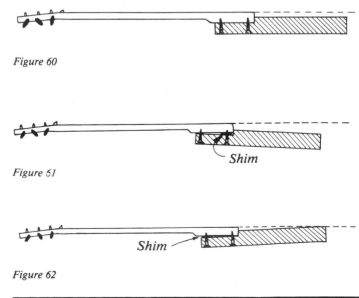

Figure 60

Figure 61

Shim

Shim

Figure 62

adjustment screw in the neckplate. *(Figure 63)* All you do in this case is loosen up the three screws. Adjust the neck angle with the adjusting screw. You need a small Allen wrench (size ⅟₁₆ ″). If you tighten the screw, turn clockwise, the neck will go backward—same effect as *Figure 61*. If you loosen it, the neck will come forward—as shown in *Figure 62*. When the neck is in a straight line with the body, as in *Figure 60*, you then tighten the bolts again.

Figure 63

STEP 8. The Strings

Some Talk about Guitar Strings

As mentioned in *Step 1*, the only way to do a good set-up is to use *new* strings. If you don't know what strings you want to put on, then the following guidelines may help:

Most strings are made of metal. An exception are the strings for classical guitars, which are made of nylon. The bass strings are metal wound around a nylon core.

Another type of string I like (for fingerpicking styles) on small body guitars (folk guitars) is the silk and steel string. It is a light gauge string and the 1st and 2nd are unwound metal. The others are wound around a core of silk. They have a lot less tension than normal steel strings, which makes them easy on your fingers. These are also good to use with old flattop guitars that don't have an x-bracing under the top. They have a more mellow sound and still good treble tones. Again, they are fine for fingerpicking styles but not so fine for rhythm playing.

Strings come in gauges or thicknesses. Strings can be bought in sets for acoustic guitars or electric guitars.

Steel strings:

acoustic guitars ⎰ heavy gauge
⎱ medium gauge ⎱ solid body
⎱ light gauge ⎰ electric guitars
⎱ extra light gauge ⎰

A rough idea of what the different gauges do for you is: the thicker the string gauge, the more volume you get. The thicker the string gauge, the higher the tension and the harder to play on your fingers. Also the heavier string gauges will demand more stress on the neck, bridge, top, and braces of your guitar. These are good to use for the rhythm playing on arch top guitars (jazz guitars). Most flattop guitars are made for medium gauge strings. It's a good all around guitar string, since you can play rhythm and also fingerpicking styles. I recommend them to people who don't know what gauge they want, or for people who play bluegrass style rhythm guitar either with or without lead breaks.

For finger pickers, light gauge strings on acoustic flattop guitars are best. They don't have as much tension and will be easy on your fingers. With light gauge strings a very low set-up is possible without the strings buzzing too much. Because most acoustic flattop guitars are built for medium gauge strings, if you want to use light gauge strings it is likely a new set-up will be necessary for your guitar. For this reason, you will lose some of the volume.

''Light gauge'' strings for solid body electric guitars are comparable to the medium gauge performance of the acoustic flattop guitar. I prefer these strings because they are light enough to play easily but you can still feel your strings. (A lot of people who play acoustic guitar as well as electric guitar like to feel the strings.) Also the strings give sufficiently and are recommended for people who don't know what gauge they want.

Extra-light gauge is usually not recommended for acoustic guitars since the volume drop is so severe. Also the guitars are not made for these strings.

This leaves us with solid body electric guitars for which these strings were originally developed. These strings are very easy on your fingers, most electric guitar players use them, and they ''bend'' very easily.

A string's sound is also determined by the material it is made of. There are nickel-wound, bronze-wound, and phosphor-bronze-wound strings. They all produce a different sound. Bronze will be a warmer, more mellow sound than nickel-wound. I very much like the warm phosphor-bronze sound. But, of course, you'll have to try it yourself.

Preference also goes for brands. The reason that I haven't mentioned any brands is because I would give you brand names I like, but that's an individual taste and so I leave it to you to try them all out.

Don't put any steel strings on a classical guitar; it isn't built for them. If you really have to do it, maybe for a little while, use the silk and steel strings.

How to Put on New Steel Strings

1. Put the string through its hole in the bridge. *(Figure 64)* Put bridge pin in place.

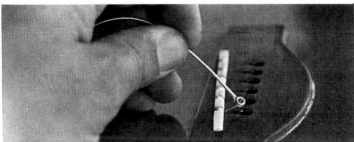

Figure 64

2. Stand behind your peghead.

3. Turn your tuner so that the hole where the string will go is positioned in a left-to-right manner (you cannot look through the hole from your position. *(Figure 65)*

4. Take the end of the string and put it through the hole on the inside. *(Figure 65)*

5. Put it far enough through the hole so that you have enough slack in the string to let it go around the tuner about two or three times. (Usually you can take two or three fingers between the string and the fingerboard to find enough slack.) *(Figure 66)* Try out what works for you.

6. Make sure the string will not slip by holding it securely in your left hand. Take the loose end in your right hand and bend it sharply toward you. *(Figure 67)*

7. Keep bending it around and go under the string. *(Figure 68)*

8. You then bend the string end straight up and toward you. This way it will clamp itself between the strings and the tuner. *(Figure 69)*

9. Now turn the tuner until the string has the right tension and tune to pitch. Make sure that you hold onto the string end so it won't slip while you are tuning. *(Figures 70 and 71)*

10. Now take the string end and wriggle it about until it breaks off. *(Figure 72)* The result is a neat and very well strung guitar. *(Figure 73)*

Note: If you do a set-up, don't break off the string end yet. Wait until you've completely finished the set-up, because you may have to loosen the strings again.

Figure 65

Figure 66

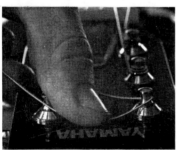

Figure 67

Figure 68

Figure 69

Figure 70

Figure 71

Figure 72

Figure 73

STEP 9. Relief

The neck of a guitar with strings strung up to pitch always
has to have a little hollow bow so the string has room to
vibrate. This "room" or space is called *relief. (Figure 74)*
(Relief should not be mistaken with another term, the so-
called "action.") If the neck is perfectly straight the strings
will, when you are playing, touch the frets at several places
(usually around the 4th and 5th fret) and cause buzzing,
which is not wanted.

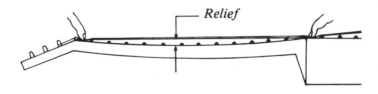

Relief

Figure 74

We check the relief as follows:

1. Hold the guitar as if you were playing.
2. With the index finger of your left hand (right hand if
you are a left handed player) press the 6th string (low E
string) in the space between the nut and the first fret.
3. You then press the same string with the little finger of
your right hand in the space between the 12th and 13th fret.
(Figure 75) This is where the neck is glued to the body. (A
lot of flattop guitars have necks with a neck joint at the
14th fret; in that case you can use the fret between the 14th
and 15th fret.) **Electric guitars** have the neck joined to the
body at the 17th fret or more. Disregard this for a moment
and use the space between the 12th and 13th fret. Now
you've made a straight line between the 1st and 12th (or
14th) fret. *(Figures 74 and 75)* You can now see if the string
touches the frets. **There should be be a small space between
the string and the frets,** with the largest space in the middle
of the neck (around the 5th and 6th fret). If this is not the

case, then your neck may happen to be exactly straight, but will most likely have a back bow.

Figure 75

4. Keep the left index finger on the 1st fret to *feel* if there is a space and use your right-hand thumb while your little finger is still at the 12th or 14th fret. Now tap the string with your thumb around the 5th or 6th fret. If there is any space at all you will hear the string tap the fret. *(Figure 76)*

Figure 76

5. With an electric guitar you repeat this procedure once more with the little finger of your right hand pressed into the last space of your fingerboard. With your thumb you check the relief by tapping at the 12th fret.

6. Using the same method, check the relief with all other strings. The relief of the low E-string needs to be larger than that of the high E-string, because the low E-string needs more room to vibrate.

I do not believe that there is a relief measurement to fit all kinds of guitars nor all different kinds of set-ups. I adjust the necks so that the relief is the smallest possible before the string starts buzzing. The rest you can adjust with the "action." Remember "action" and "relief" are two different things. We adjust the relief by tightening or loosening the nut of the adjustable trussrod, provided there is one. Otherwise, the heatset mentioned earlier will become necessary. If the neck is too hollow, then tighten the nut. If the neck is bent backwards then loosen the nut (see *Step 5.* Straightening the Neck). Again, be careful. A quarter turn of the nut is often enough.

Note: The trussrod can only adjust the neck between the nut and the 12th fret, and cannot adjust the angle the guitar neck makes with the guitar body. *(Figure 21)*

If you have done all procedures in *Step 5* then your neck should be straight. Once the strings are added and tuned to pitch I have found that most of the time their tension will bend the neck enough to give it the correct relief.

STEP 10. Action

Now that we have adjusted the neck, the next step is to adjust the guitar so it can be played as easily as possible. Here is where we get to the term **action.** *(Figure 77)* It does not only mean how high the strings are from the fingerboard.

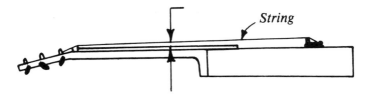

Figure 77

In fact, action is the resistance of a string when you press it down. This resistance depends on the distance from the string to the fingerboard and the tension of the string. The tension of the string depends on the thickness and the material of the string (metal strings have a much higher tension than nylon strings). However, many guitar repairmen and also guitar manufacturers will tell you that there has to be a specific space measurement between the strings and the fretboard. For instance, Fender's string height specification, using Fender's 150 standard rock'n roll strings, for easy action is:

top of 1st Fret to string: 0.020 $\quad \begin{array}{l} +0.05 \\ -0.08 \end{array}$ inch

top of 12th Fret to string: 0.065 $\quad +0.01$ inch

So you cannot speak about action in general without mentioning the kind of strings. As soon as (in the above example) you are using other strings, the string height specifications will not be the same anymore. This is the reason I don't bother with certain specifications. Especially because every guitar player has his/her own ideas of what an easy playing guitar is. Also it depends on your individual style. A fingerpicking style player will often want to have an action as low as possible and not even mind a little rattling or buzzing of the strings. A rhythm guitar player or bluegrass flatpicker will prefer a much higher action since he/she will be hitting the strings much harder. In this case he/she may want a little more relief also.

The higher the strings are above the fretboard, the harder it will be to play. Also the more tension the string has, the harder it will be to play.

The lower the strings are to the fretboard the easier it is to play and the more "true" your notes will be in the higher positions.

So the *action* has to do with:

1. The kind of strings you are using.
2. Saddle
3. Bridge
4. Nut

You will have to adjust the action in this order, providing (again) that the neck angle is correct.

STEP 11. Check Saddle Height

Acoustic guitars with non-adjustable saddles. (Figure 78)

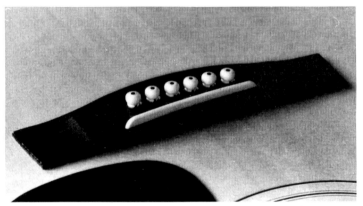

Figure 78

For the best performance the saddle should rise out above the bridge about ⅓ of its own height. To find this, loosen your strings and take the strings out of the saddle. Then take a pencil and draw a line on the saddle at the point where it sticks out of the bridge. *(Figure 79)* The saddle should be easy to take out. It should not be glued. You may have to use some pliers if it is really tight in the bridge. Always pull straight upward. When the saddle is out you can now see and measure how far it sticks out compared to its own height. *(Figures 80 and 83)* To adjust saddle height see *Step 12.*

Figure 79   Figure 80

Acoustic guitars with adjustable saddles (Figures 81, 82a, and 82b)

The adjustaable saddle for flattop guitars *(Figures 82a and 82b)* consists of two pieces:

1. A metal saddle support piece with a slot on the top

side and two adjusting screws at each end.

2. The plastic or bone saddle. If you have a guitar with this kind of saddle then you want the plastic or bone saddle to stick out of the metal support piece not more than one-half its own height.

For electric guitars

Since all saddles form a unity with the bridge and all are adjustable in height there is no general standard on how high it should be.

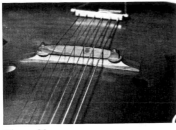
Figure 81

Figure 82a

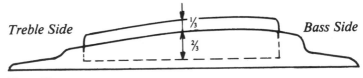
Figure 82b

STEP 12. Adjust the Saddle.

For acoustic guitars with non-adjustable saddles.

In general, if you want to lower the strings on your guitar for easier playing all yuou have to do is lower the saddle. As mentioned before, it should stick out of the bridge not more than about ⅓ of its own height. *(Figure 83)* Loosen your strings and take the strings out of the saddle. Next take the saddle out of the bridge.

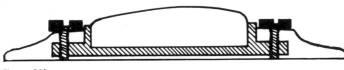

Treble Side   ⅓ ⅔   Bass Side

Figure 83

1. First check the contour of the saddle with a contour guide. If your fingerboard is slightly contoured or arched then the top of your saddle should have the same shape. *(Figures 84a and 84b)*

If your fingerboard is arched and your saddle is not, then you have to make an arch on your saddle. Take the contour guide (available at any hardware store) and press it over the top of the fingerboard at the widest end of the fingerboard. *(Figure 84a)* Next draw this arch on your saddle with a

Figure 84a

Figure 84b

pencil, as close to the top as possible. *(Figure 85)* Since the saddle will be longer than the shape of your fingerboard, you have to position the contour guide in the middle of the saddle. The line you draw will give you enough guidance in order to shape the ends of the saddle top. The saddle should be a little higher on the bass side than on the treble side. *(Figure 86)*

Figure 85

Treble Side   Bass Side

Figure 86

2. Now file the saddle in that proposed shape. *(Figure 87)* While you are sanding or filing, make sure that at the same time you create a slight backward slant *(Figure 88)* to prevent the strings from buzzing. This will also serve to guide the string to the string hole in the bridge. Most of the time the top of the bridge is arched. In that case you can usually follow the arched line of the bridge so the top line of the saddle is parallel to the top line of the bridge. *(Figure 89)* Check if the treble side is indeed lower than the bass side. If not, adjust the saddle so this will be the case. When you've finished shaping the saddle, sand the scratches off with fine sandpaper and polish with steel wool. **Do Not make notches in the top of the saddle to guide the strings. Note:** When the top of the saddle is worn (small notches) this can be the cause of a "buzzing" sound. If this is the case, follow the previous steps to file or sand out these notches.

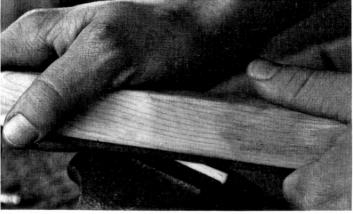

Figure 87

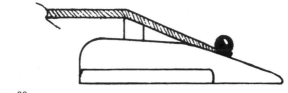

Figure 88

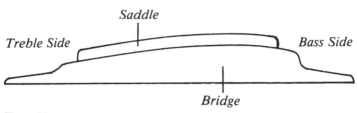

Saddle

Treble Side   Bass Side

Bridge

Figure 89

3. To **lower** the saddle, just file or sand off a part of **the bottom.** To be sure you take off the proper amount, draw a straight line designating where you want to file to on the saddle. *(Figure 90)* Be sure you don't take off too much. It is better to do it a few times and come out with the correct height than to find that you've taken off a fraction too much.

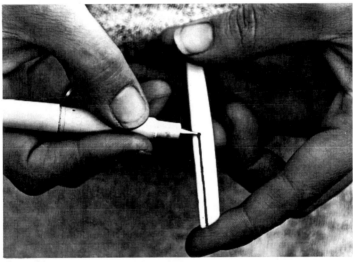

Figure 90

4. If you want to *raise* the saddle, you have a choice. The best one is to make a new saddle. Make it out of a piece of bone or buy a saddle blank in a music store or from a repairman. Preferably don't buy a cheap plastic one because they are not very good. To make a new saddle, you have to cut it to the right length first. Round off the ends. Then you have to file or sand the saddle to the correct thickness so it will fit snugly, but not tightly, in the saddle slot. For the next steps follow the procedure as described before.

The other choice is to raise it by putting shims underneath. If you have to raise the whole saddle, you cut a shim (thin piece of hard wood or plastic) in the shape of the saddle slot and as thick as you want the saddle to raise, and lay it in the saddle slot to support the full length of the saddle. You can also glue a piece of hardwood, plastic, or bone to the bottom of the saddle. It goes as follows:

a. Glue a shim of about ⅛ " thick to the bottom of the saddle with "Krazy Glue." The shim needs to be a little larger than the size of the saddle. *(Figure 91)*

b. When the glue has dried, file off the excess material so that it is all flush with the saddle. *(Figure 92)*

c. Insert the saddle in the saddle slot and check the saddle height. If the saddle is too high you have to file some off the bottom as described before. If you only have to raise the bass side or the treble side, you cut a shorter piece which you put under the side of the saddle that needs to be raised. I would only suggest this as a temporary solution.

Figure 91   *Figure 92*

Acoustic guitars with adjustable saddles.

Arch top guitars, acoustic as well as electric, have a bridge consisting of two pieces. The upper piece houses the saddle and is only adjustable in height. *(Figure 81)* The whole thing is held in place by the downward pressure of the strings.

In case your guitar has a bridge and saddle like those shown in *Figures 82a and 82b,* make sure the saddle bone does not stick out too much (not more than half its own height). If it does, file or sand some off the bottom of the saddle. Also check if the saddle doesn't move in the slot. If it does, your saddle is too thin and you'll need to replace it with one that fits. This saddle too is only adjustable in height.

You can adjust the saddle height by turning the adjustment rings. You can raise or lower the entire saddle or just the bass side or treble side.

Note: The best thing to do if you have a saddle as shown in *Figure 82a* is to take the saddle and adjustable metal part out and convert it to a solid non-adjustable saddle. *See "Adjust the Saddle Slot,"* page 55. In addition, you'll need to make a new saddle as described before.

Ovation guitars

The saddle of acoustic/electric Ovation guitars *(Figure 93)* is adjustable in height by means of shims underneath the saddle. The shims come with the guitar.

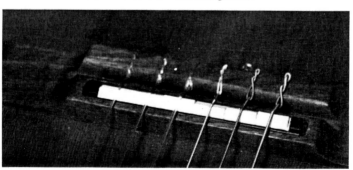

Figure 93

For electric guitars

The saddle and bridge are usually one piece with electric guitars. A few basic type bridges are consistently used. These are what I call the "Gibson" type bridges *(Figures 94a and 94b)* and "Fender" type bridges *(Figures 95a and 95b).*

The Gibson Type saddle height can be adjusted with a big screwdriver. On both sides of the saddle/bridge are adjusting screws which are also the saddle supports. You can either adjust the whole saddle by adjusting both the screws or just one side by adjusting one screw. (Some bridges have adjusting wheels instead of screws.)

The Fender Type bridge has three *(Figure 95a)* or six separate saddles *(Figure 95b)* adjustable in height with two small adjusting screws in each saddle. When you have a bridge with three separate saddles, then each saddle supports two strings *(Figure 95a)*. Here you need an Allen wrench, size $\frac{1}{16}''$, to adjust the height of the saddles.

Figure 94a

Figure 94b

Figure 95a

Figure 95b

Make sure they are adjusted in an arched fashion like the fingerboard. *(Figure 96)* Try it out by playing. Practice some finger runs in the 10th-12th fret area from the 1st string to the 6th string making sure you don't "stumble" over one string to the next. If you can go smoothly from the 1st to the 6th and back then you have it right. If there is any buzzing then raise the particular string a little more. Keeping this in mind, after adjusting one string you may have to adjust the other five strings again, so your fingering can stay smooth, thus maintaining that important arch I mentioned. It's just a matter of trial and error until you get it how you want it.

The other Fender Type bridge has six separate saddles. *(Figure 95b)* Each saddle supports and guides one string. Every string can be adjusted to its own ideal height by adjusting the two small adjustment screws in each saddle. You need an Allen wrench of $\frac{1}{16}''$ to do the job. Here also you have to make sure that you adjust the saddles in an arched manner that resembles the arched shape of the fingerboard, so you won't "stumble" onto strings when fingering from one string to another. *(Figure 97)*

Note: If it happens that, after you have adjusted the saddles to the right height, the strings touch the pickup(s) all you have to do is lower the pickup(s). You will find an adjusting screw at each side of the pickup. Lower it by turning the screws counterclockwise. *(Figure 95b)* The closer the pickup to the string, the more volume you'll get. Therefore, you can adjust the "volume balance" between high and low strings with the same screws, as the adjusting screw at the treble side will lower or raise only that side.

The same with the other screw on the bass side. A number of pickups also have adjustable poles. You screw them in or out of the pickup if you want less or more volume from that particular string. *(Figure 94a)* For further saddle adjustments see *Step 16.*

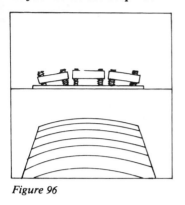

Figure 96

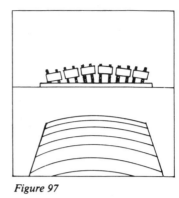

Figure 97

STEP 13. Check Bridge

Acoustic Guitars

The function of the bridge is to attach the strings (most acoustic guitars), hold the saddle, and to conduct the vibration of the strings from the saddle to the top of the guitar. The top will then vibrate and so cause the air in the guitar body to vibrate. These sound waves are amplified inside the guitar body and then come out of the sound hole. The saddle slot should be as deep as possible, leaving about $\frac{1}{16}$" wood, or a little more, under the saddle, so the bridge will conduct the vibrations from the saddle more directly. *(Figure 98)*

First check if the bridge is glued properly to the top and is not coming loose. If it is coming loose, have the bridge taken off and reglued by a professional repairman. Something to look out for is that the bridge can be too high, although this doesn't happen very often. You can check this by looking down the neck while the strings are loosened. The top of the bridge should be about 2 mm above the line of the fretboard. (This is not necessarily true for classical guitars.) *(Figure 99)* Of course, your neck should be correctly fused to the body (straight in line with the guitar top). If the neck has come up, then you may get a false idea of your saddle height. *(See Figures 60, 61 and 62)*

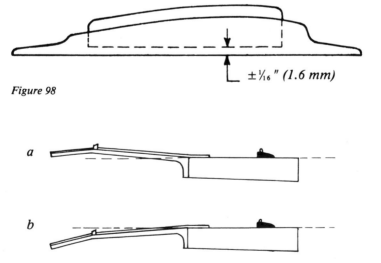

$\pm\frac{1}{16}$" *(1.6 mm)*

Figure 98

a

b

Figure 99

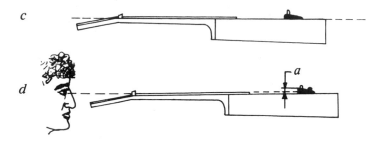

Figure 99 (continued)

Electric Guitars

Since the bridge and the saddles of electric guitars are very often one piece see *Step 11* and *Step 12*. Check if the bridge is screwed tightly to the body.

STEP 14. Bridge Adjustment

Acoustic Guitars

Bridge too high

When you've found that your bridge is too high you can lower the bridge by shaving it down. Take the following steps:

1. Loosen the strings.
2. Take bridge pins out. *(Figure 100)*
3. Take strings out. *(Figure 100)*
4. Take saddle out.
5. Protect area around bridge with cardboard. Take a piece of cardboard and in the middle cut out the shape of the bridge. *(Figure 101)*

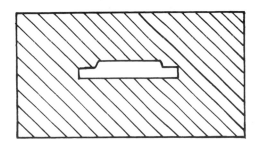

Figure 100

Figure 101

6. With scraper, file, plane, or rasp lower the bridge by taking off as much wood from the top of the bridge as necessary. *(Figure 102)*

7. Sand smooth with 100 and 250 grade sandpaper until all scratches are gone. *(Figure 103)*

8. Polish with 00 steel wool (very fine). *(Figure 104)*

9. If you've found that your bridge was stained black you have to stain it the same color again. If you've found that the wood of the bridge looks nicer without the black stain, take all the black stain off with a scraper (utility knifeblade) or sandpaper. Black leather dye is easy and cheap if you want to stain it black. *(Figure 105)* After staining, polish with steel wool, if you feel it is necessary. Finish off by rubbing on a few drops of oil (lemon or vegetable oil).

Figure 102

Figure 103

Figure 104

Figure 105

10. Recheck if saddle slot is still deep enough. The saddle should stick in the slot about ⅔ of its own height. *(See Step 11.)* Preferably the slot should be so deep that only about ¹⁄₁₆ " wood is left under the saddle. *(Figure 98)* If you want to lower the saddle see *Step 12.*

11. If the saddle slot needs to be deeper, see *Step 16.*

12. Check and fix bridge pin holes. If you've taken away some wood in the bridge pin area, you may find that your bridge pins won't fit all the way in the bridge pin holes. *(Figure 106)*

First, you must ream out the bridge pin holes a little. A tapered reamer is necessary for this job. *(Figure 107)* **Be careful!** Take off just a little bit at a time and try to fit the bridge pin after every quarter turn of the reamer. You really don't want the bridge pin all of a sudden to disappear. Do this until the pin fits snugly in the hole.

After that you can countersink the pin holes, if you want to, with an electric drill and a countersink bit or something similar. I like to use a small round grinder bit on a Dremel tool. You can use this bit also on an electric drill. *(Figure 108)*

Now your bridge pins fit correctly in the holes. *(Figure 109)*

Bridge too low

If your bridge is too low, it will neet to be replaced with a new bridge. See your guitar repairman.

Figure 106

Figure 107

Figure 108

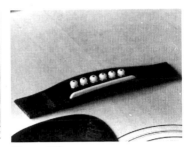

Figure 109

The saddle slot

Step 16 shows how to make a new saddle slot in a bridge or make the old one deeper. This technique is necessary when you want to:

a. Deepen the old saddle slot.

b. Make a new saddle slot to adjust intonation.

c. Convert an adjustable saddle into a solid non-adjustable saddle.

d. Convert a guitar for lefthanded use.

A loose bridge

When you've found that the bridge is coming off the guitar top, it then needs to be removed and reglued. This is a repair job and I will not describe it here.

Adjust bridge of electric guitars

See *Step 12.* "Adjust the Saddle Height for Electric Guitars" and *Step 16.* "Adjust Intonation Of Electric Guitars."

STEP 15. Check Nut/Adjust Nut

Figure 110

Nuts are made of bone, brass, plastic, and even wood. The purpose of the nut is to space the strings an equal distance from each other and (if you don't have a zero fret) to also determine the height of the strings above the fingerboard. In case you do have a zero fret *(Figure 110)*, which really is a better system but strangely enough is seldom used, then the height of the string is determined by the zero fret, which should be the same height as the other frets. For this reason the string height will be as perfect as you can ever get it. Since most guitars don't utilize a zero fret, then it is the nut which needs to determine the string height.

How to check for correct string height

You check for the correct string height by pressing each string between the 2nd and 3rd fret, while the guitar is tuned to pitch. The ideal is when the string just clears the top of the 1st fret. *(Figure 111)* If the distance is greater than that, you have to lower the string slots which will be described on the next page. If there is no distance, then the string slot in the nut is too low. In that case the nut should be replaced. Don't use plastic nuts because they are hollow and have no mass to help the string vibration (sustain). However, if you don't want to replace the nut you can take out the nut as described before on page 23 and glue a shim to the bottom with "Krazy Glue" or other brand of cyanoacetate glue.

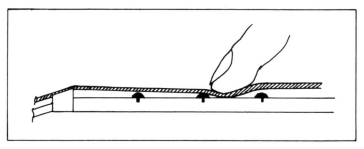

Figure 111

How to raise the nut

1. First clean off the nut *(Figure 112)*, then

2. Glue a shim of about ⅛ " thick to the bottom of the nut. The shim needs to be a little larger than the size of the nut. Use bone, plastic, or hard wood as material for the shim. *(Figure 113)*

3. When the glue has dried, file off the excess material until it is almost flush with the nut. *(Figure 114)* When you have the material almost filed off, you can scrape the last bit with a sharp utility knife blade, so you won't have file marks all over the nut. *(Figure 115)*

4. Clean up the area where the nut will be glued in place. *(Figure 116)*

5. Glue the modified nut back in place with a drop or two of "Krazy Glue." *(Figure 117)*

6. Put strings back in place and tune to pitch.

7. Now re-check the string height. *(Figure 111)* The space between the string and the top of the 1st fret is now probably too much. (Any space that is larger than the space needed to clear the 1st fret is too much.) When re-checking the string height, you most likely will find that the string and thus the nut is too high; lower the string by filing down that string slot in the nut. Use needle files or even hacksaw blades, or if you have them, jeweler saw blades. There are also nut files you can buy, like the ones I use in *Figure 119*.

They are not cheap but very convenient. Also you can simply fold a piece of sandpaper and deepen the slot with a sawing motion. This will take some time, but on the other hand, once the nut is adjusted correctly you will never have to bother with it again.

In any case, be very careful that you don't make the slot too deep (check over and over again after every few sanding motions) and also do not sand it too wide. Actually you don't want the string slot to be wider than the particular string. So you see it's a very delicate operation. Take your time!

Figure 112   *Figure 113*

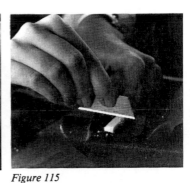

Figure 114   *Figure 115*

Figure 116   *Figure 117*

The string slot deepening procedure

1. Check string height while string is tuned to pitch. *(Figure 111)*

2. Loosen string a bit and remove it from the string slot. *(Figure 118)*

3. Protect your headstock and fingerboard with some layers of masking tape.

4. File, saw, or sand the slot a little. You have to file downward in the direction of and parallel with the headstock so the string slot will be slanted. *(Figure 119)*

5. Put the string back in the slot, tune to pitch, and check string height again.

6. If still too high, keep repeating procedure until the right height for each string is achieved. You will then have the situation as shown in *Figure 120*.

7. Since we want the depth of the string slots in the nut to be one-half the diameter of the string it supports *(Figure 121),* we will have to file off the excess, if there is any.

8. Loosen all strings and take them out of the nut slots. Put three strings on one side and three on the other side. *(Figure 122)*

9. With a pencil, draw a line over the length of the fret so that half the string diameter will be under the line. *(Figure 122)* Do this also on the other side of the nut, so you will have some guidance when filing the excess.

10. Now file off the excess material on top of the drawn line. *(Figure 123)* Finish the job with some fine sandpaper and steel wool.

Note: Make sure that all the bottoms of the nut slots are refiled/sanded so that you won't stumble over the strings when fingering from one string to another. Actually, if done correctly, you will wind up in a slightly arched line (like your fretboard). *(Figure 124)*

Figure 118

Figure 119

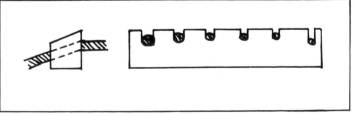

Figure 120

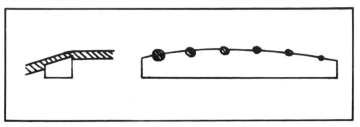

Figure 121

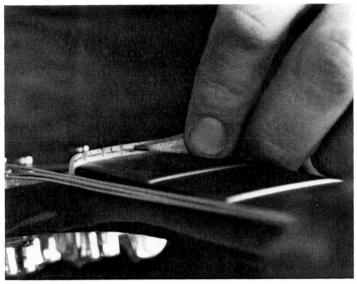

Figure 122

Figure 123

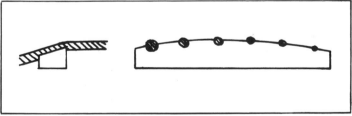

Figure 124

How to make a new nut

Making a new nut is not an easy job. All I can say about making it is to copy your old nut as closely as you can. If you have one, a belt sander can be a great help. Keep the following steps in mind:

1. Buy or make a nut blank, preferably of bone.

2. Thin down the nut blank so it will fit tightly in the nut slot. *(Figure 125)*

3. Make the bottom flush with the bottom of the headstock if necessary. *(Figure 126)* Adjust to your own guitar.

4. Put nut blank in nut slot *(Figure 127)* and with a pencil make marks where to sand it flush on the sides. Mark on the front, bottom, and on the back and top of the nut. *(Figure 128)*

5. File off excess on each side so the nut will now be flush with the neck. *(Figure 129)*

6. Glue the nut in place with a few drops of "Krazy Glue." *(Figure 130)*

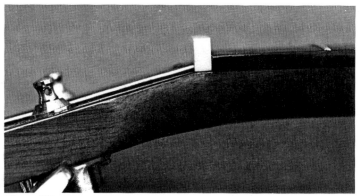

Figure 125

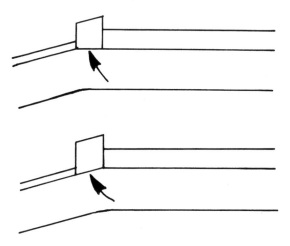

Figure 126

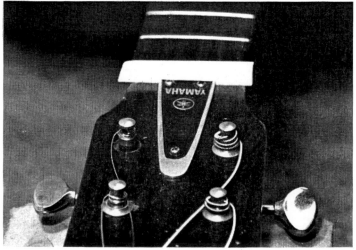

Figure 127

Figure 128

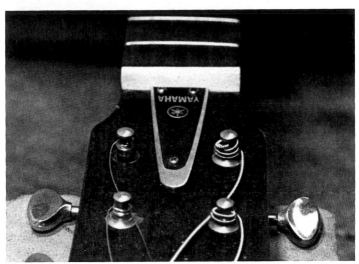

Figure 129

Figure 130

7. Mark off where you want the outside E (low and high) strings to be. ¾₂″ (2, 4 mm) on each side usually does very well. *(Figure 131)* Use a rule with ⅟₃₂″ readings.

8. Then measure the distance between these marks. *(Figure 132)* You don't need to use a caliper as shown in the photograph; your ruler with ⅟₃₂″ readings is accurate enough.

9. Divide the distance found by five and you come up with all the spaces between the strings.

10. Mark these spaces on the nut with a pencil. The marks are the places of the nut slots. *(Figure 133)*

11. Check if the marks are evenly spaced, then file the slots *(Figure 134)* and finish off as described in the slot deepening process. *(Figures 118 through 124)*

Note: If you have a zero fret then you don't have to be so careful with the depth of the string slots in the nut. As long as the slots are lower than the top of the zero fret you are O.K. The nut merely acts here as a spacer for the strings. *(Figure 135)*

Figure 131

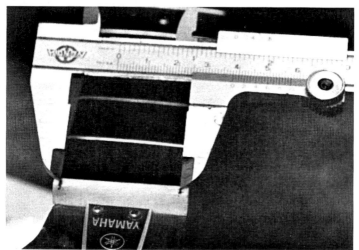

Figure 132

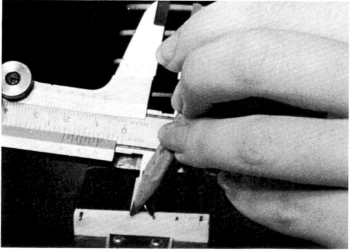

Figure 133

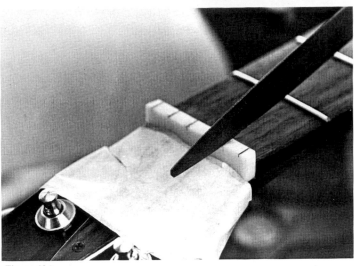

Figure 134

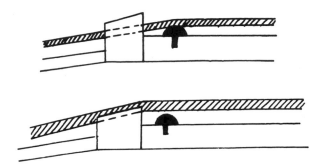

Figure 135

STEP 16. Compensation of the Saddle

The scale length of the guitar is the theoretical length of the string between the nut (or top of zero fret) and the saddle. The 12th fret is **always exactly half** this distance. (Figure 136)

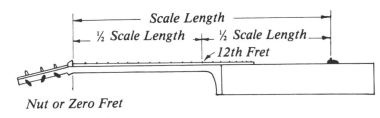

Figure 136

The distance from the nut to the 12th fret is the same as the distance from the 12th fret to the saddle. Theoretically this is true. However, the string needs to be a certain height above the fingerboard. To play, you have to press down the string over a small distance. This will stretch the string and cause it to have a greater tension. In other words, the note you will hear will be a little higher than the note you want to hear. This note will be off more and more the farther you go down the fingerboard. This is an adjustment situation. To compensate for this "built-in" fault, the saddle needs to be re-adjusted. In essence, it means that the theoretical scale-length will need to be made a little longer.

So actually the distance between the 12th fret and the saddle will be made a little longer than the distance between the nut and the 12th fret. *(Figure 137)*

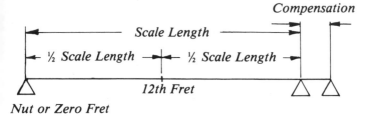

Compensation

Nut or Zero Fret

Figure 137

Since the amount of compensation depends on the tension of the string* and the distance from the string to the fingerboard, the bass string (6th string) whose distance from the fingerboard is greater and has greater tension, needs more compensation than the high E string (1st string). The 1st string is closer to the fingerboard and employs less tension. This is the reason saddles are not put in parallel to the front line of the bridge but are instead manufactured with a slight slant. *(Figure 138)*

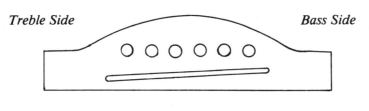

Top View

Figure 138

Note: Since the tension in the six strings of classical guitars does not vary much, the difference between the compensation of the high string and the low string is usually ignored. That's why classical guitars usually have their saddles parallel to the edge of the bridge. *(Figure 139)*
Finding the right amount of compensation is called "setting the intonation."
(Webster's definition: "The manner of producing tones with regard to accurate pitch")

Figure 139

*Here you will understand that heavy gauge strings need more compensation than medium gauge strings and medium gauge strings need more compensation than light gauge strings.

Check and Adjust Intonation (or Bridge Compensation)

Electric and acoustic

I like to start with the electric guitars. Some electric guitars have so-called compensated saddles, for instance, archtop guitars and most Gibson guitars. *(Figure 140)* There is nothing you can do here to adjust each string length separately because they just do not adjust. The only thing you can do, if you find that the intonation is not right, is to adjust the saddle by moving the whole bridge forward or backward (for archtop guitars) or adjust the saddle by moving it backward or forward with the small adjustment screws on the back side of each pole (Gibson bridge, *Figure 140*). However, this can never be a very accurate adjustment since you move several strings at the same time. The only thing you can do, if you want to be able to adjust the intonation of each string perfectly, is to replace the bridge with one that has adjustable saddles. Still, nowadays, most of the bridges of electric guitars have adjustable saddles for each separate string.

I like to go back to the three types of adjustable bridges I mentioned earlier which are good representatives of all the electric guitar bridges.

Figure 140

The "Gibson" type and the "Fender" type bridges

The Gibson bridge, with adjustable saddle, is called "Tune O Matic." It has six individual saddles adjustable in length. A small screwdriver is needed to adjust each saddle. *(Figure 141)*

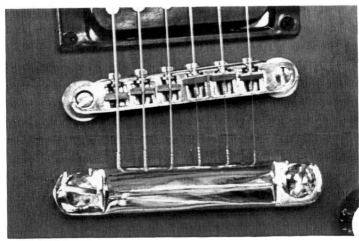

Figure 141

The original "Fender" type bridges (Music Master, Telecaster, etc.) have three adjustable saddle pieces. Each saddle supports two strings. So, you must "adjust" two strings at the same time. In other words, you'll never be able to set the intonation of each string perfectly. Instead find a distance that is satisfactory for both strings on the saddle. You may have to compromise. Use a small Philips screwdriver to do the adjustment. *(Figures 142 and 95a)*

The other "Fender" type bridge (*i.e.* Stratocaster) has six fully adjustable saddles. Here a small screwdriver is needed to make the adjustments lengthwise. *(Figures 143 and 95b)*

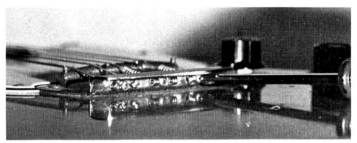

Figure 142

Figure 143

Note: Check your own bridge to find out what kind and what size screwdriver you will need.

To check and adjust the intonation, with one string at a time, proceed as follows:

1. The volume knobs full open
2. The tone knobs one-half open
3. Turn on only one pick-up. If you have a choice, use the one nearest the fretboard.
4. Make sure the other strings won't vibrate by setting a piece of foam plastic under the strings. *(Figure 144)*

Figure 144

5. Tune string to pitch.

6. Press the string just before the 12th fret. *(Figure 145)*

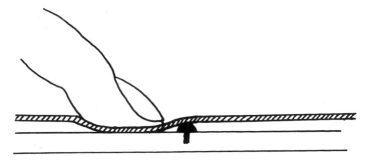

12th Fret

Figure 145

7. Pluck the string softly in the middle, between your finger and the bridge.

8. Compare the tone with the harmonic above the 12th fret. *(Figure 146)* The harmonic is made by gently placing the top of your left index finger exactly above the 12th fret on the string, then pressing lightly but not pushing the string down. It might take some practice. Plucking the string softly with your other finger should get you a clear tone which is the harmonic of that particular string.

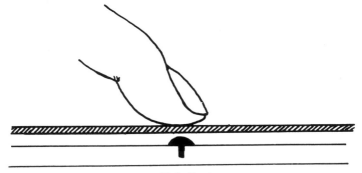

12th Fret

Figure 146

9. If the fretted tone is lower than the harmonic, then you must move the saddle a little forward until both notes are exactly the same. You can use your ears to do this, but a strobotuner or other electronic tuner would be best for accuracy. *(Figure 147a)*

Figure 147a

10. If the fretted note is higher than the harmonic then keep moving the saddle backward until both notes are the same.

You may have to repeat steps 5–10 because once the saddle is moved you will have to tune the string exactly to pitch again.

Work every string this way. The whole procedure is useful only when you *use new strings*.

Adjusting the intonation of an acoustic guitar is quite a different story. Here the saddle compensation is a figure found only by experience and try outs. In general, it can be said that for steel strings, compensation on the treble side is $\frac{1}{32}$″ to $\frac{1}{16}$″ and on the bass side it is $\frac{1}{8}$″ to $\frac{3}{16}$″. Classical guitars measure $\frac{1}{32}$″ to $\frac{1}{16}$″.

I cannot give precise measurements because the compensation depends on string height, string tension, and scale length unique to every guitar.

On steel string acoustic guitars I prefer $\frac{1}{16}$″ (1, 6 mm) on the treble side and $\frac{5}{32}$″ (4 mm) on the bass side. This setting becomes the front line of the saddle. *(Figure 148)* Check your intonation the same way as you do an electric guitar as described in points 4 through 8. *(See also Figure 147b)*

Now, in the particular case with acoustics (and classicals) where we cannot adjust every separate string, we have to compromise and go for "as close as possible." So if you find that your intonation is very close, just leave it that way. If the intonation is way off, then you will probably want to improve it. We do this by adjusting the saddle slot.

Figure 147b

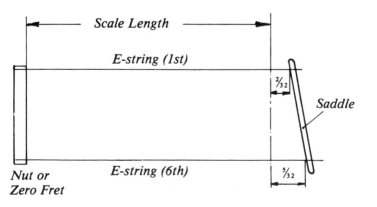

Figure 148

Adjust the saddle slot

First you will have to fill in the old saddle slot with a piece of wood and then make a new saddle slot. Tools you will need for this job are:

- 2 clamps
- 1 (Dremel) moto tool with router attachment or similar machine *(Figure 149)*
- 1 router guide *(Figure 150)* You make this one your self according to the drawing. Make sure you have straight edges on the inside of the guide.
- 1 Dremel router bit No. 193
- 1 white pencil
- 1 measuring stick, long enough to measure ½ the scale length
- 1 small ruler with ⅟₃₂ " readings

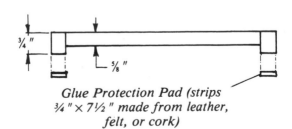

Figure 149

Top View

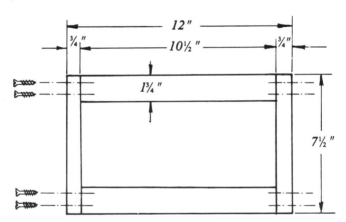

*Glue Protection Pad (strips
¾ " × 7½ " made from leather,
felt, or cork)*

*To assemble the four pieces
use (wood) glue and screws*

Front View

Figure 150

How to fill in the saddle slot

    1. Take off the strings.

    2. Protect area around bridge with a piece of cardboard out of which you have cut the shape of the saddle. Any caps can be filled with masking tape. *(Figure 151)*

    3. Take the saddle out of the bridge.

    4. Make a copy of the saddle out of a piece of hardwood, preferably the same wood as the bridge is constructed of (brown/red =rosewood; black =ebony). First scrape the bridge a little to find out if the bridge is rosewood that has been stained black. Make sure the wood fits precisely in the saddle slot. This is really not so difficult; it works exactly as making a new saddle, as shown in *Step 12.*

    5. Glue the piece of wood in the saddle slot. (Titebond, epoxy, or "Krazy Glue"—any of these will do the job.) *(Figure 152)*

    6. File and/or scrape off any excess wood that sticks out of the bridge. *(Figure 153a)* Then finish it off with fine sandpaper and steel wool. *(Figure 153b)* If you've done the job right, the whole operation will barely be visible. *(Figure 154)*

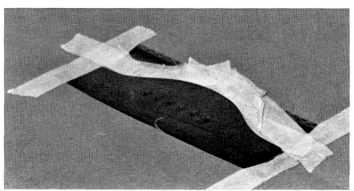

Figure 151

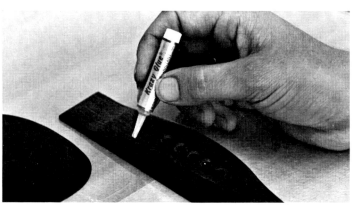

Figure 152

Figure 153 a

Figure 153b

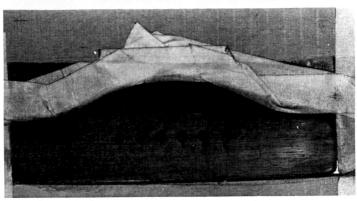

Figure 154

How to find the new position of the saddle slot

We are now going to mark where our new saddle slot will be. You must work very precisely here.

1. Measure the distance from the front of the nut (or the top of the zero fret, if you have one) to the top of the 12th fret. With a pencil, mark the point at the 12th fret on your measuring stick. *(Figure 155)*

2. Now you move the measurement that you've just found over to the 12th fret and bridge. Position the end that you held at the nut exactly above the middle of the 12th fret. The other end will automatically end up on top of the bridge. *(Figure 156)* Mark the point you've found on the stick on the bridge with a pencil. *(Figure 156)*

Figure 155

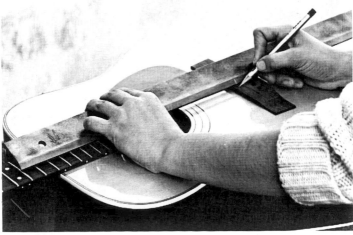

Figure 156

3. Draw a line through this point parallel with the front line of the bridge. *(Figure 157)*

4. Mark the points carefully with a pencil where the outside strings would cross this line. *(Figure 158)*

5. Take a ruler with ¹⁄₃₂" readings and measure ²⁄₃₂" (1.6 mm) on this line toward the bridgepin holes and mark this point carefully. *(Figure 159)*

6. Measure and mark ⁵⁄₃₂" (4 mm) at the bass side. *(Figure 159)*

7. Draw a straight line between these new found points. Let the line stick out a little on each side of these points. How much they have to stick out depends on the length of your saddle. *(Figure 160)* Now you have found the new position of the saddle slot. *(Figure 161)* The line is the front line of the saddle slot.

Figure 157

Figure 158

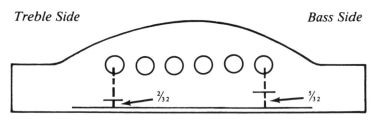

Treble Side   Bass Side

Top View

Figure 159

Figure 160

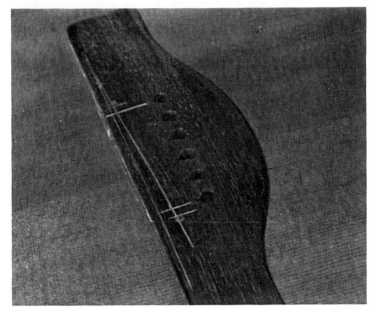

Figure 161

Making the saddle slot

1. Place the router guide *(Figure 150)* over the bridge and clamp very gently with the two clamps so that the guide can still be moved. *(Figure 162)* Make sure you protect the back of the guitar from damage by the clamps.

2. Adjust the height of the moto tool's router attachment in its highest position, so the router bit will not touch the bridge. *(Figure 163)*

3. Set the Dremel moto tool on top of your router guide. *(Figure 164)*

4. Place one side of the moto tool base plate against the router guide. *(Figure 164)*

5. Lower the router bit until it almost touches the wood on the bridge. *(Figure 165)*

6. Line up the router guide with the line of the saddle slot. Make sure that you keep the router base against the router guide when doing this! You move the router guide until the router bit is situated over the treble side of the new saddle line. *(Figure 165)* Now clamp the router guide tightly on that side. Adjust the other side of the router guide by sliding the moto tool from the treble side to the bass side. *(Figures 166 and 167)* Adjust the router guide so that the router bit follows exactly the line of the saddle. Once you have established this point, clamp this side of the router guide. Check if the router bit follows the line exactly. You may have to make some more adjustments.

7. When lined up, clamp the router guide tightly to the guitar top.

8. Now make your saddle slot by making a number of passes each about $\frac{1}{16}''$ deep.

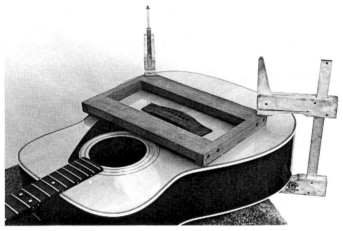

Figure 162

Figure 163

Figure 164

Figure 165

Figure 166

Figure 167

The first pass:
  a) Lower the router bit by adjusting the router attachment of your moto tool until it touches the wood of the bridge.
  b) Take away the moto tool, then lower $\frac{1}{16}$" more.
  c) Turn on the power of the moto tool.
  d) While keeping in touch with the router guide, lower the dremel tool in a straight line.
  e) Make the pass. *(Figures 166 and 167)*
  f) *Switch off the power and wait until the moto tool stops turning!*
  g) Now lift the moto tool straight up.
  h) Clean the wood dust from the saddle slot.

The next passes:
Repeat the procedure of the first pass as many times as needed, making each pass $\frac{1}{16}$" deeper than the previous one until the remaining wood under the new saddle slot is $+\frac{1}{16}$" (1.6 mm). You can find this by measuring the height of the bridge on the outside *(Figure 168)* and the depth of the saddle slot *(Figure 169)*. By subtracting these two figures you will find the actual thickness of the remaining wood under the saddle slot.

9. When you have finished, sand off the pencil lines with fine sandpaper and/or steel wool. *(Figure 170)*

10. Insert the saddle and the job is done. *(Figure 171)*

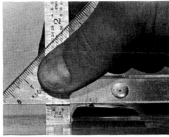

Figure 168

Figure 169

Figure 170

Figure 171

CHAPTER V

How to Adjust a Guitar for Lefthanded Use

It is quite easy to adjust an electric guitar for lefthanded use. Just reverse the strings and adjust the intonation, as described before. Then make a new nut since you have to reverse the slots in the nut. For acoustic guitars you will have to follow the same route as for compensating the saddle. Only this time, reverse the bass and treble side. *(Figure 172)* Thus:

1. Fill in the old saddle slot with a piece of wood. (See "How To Make A New Saddle")

2. Find the line where your new saddle is going to be, only now reverse the base and treble side. (See "Adjust The Saddle Slot")

3. Router your new saddle slot as described before. Here, too, you will have to make a new nut because you have to reverse the string slots.

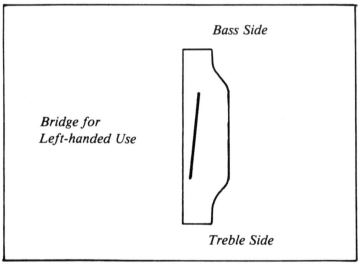

Figure 172

If you have a pick guard on your guitar, it will now be upside down. My advice is do *not* try to remove it. Many manufacturers (for example, Martin) don't lacquer the guitar top underneath the pick guard. So if you must have a pick guard, just make an extra one out of plastic or wood veneer and glue it with contact cement opposite the old one. *(Figure 173)*

This is it! It probably has taken a lot of effort and concentration in the beginning, but once you begin to understand the logic in the order of the steps, and after some more experience, you will be able to check and perfectly adjust your guitar in a short time.

I hope that this book and working on your guitar yourself has added to your knowledge about the guitar.

To play it now is up to you.

Figure 173

The Most Common Causes of Buzzing and What to Do about It

1.	Strings not tuned to pitch	Tune to pitch
2.	Old strings	Replace old strings
3.	Loose frets	Fix loose frets
4.	Uneven frets	Dress frets
5.	Neck has twisted (warped)	See professional repairman
6.	Not enough or no relief in neck	Adjust relief
7.	Set-screws loose in tuning peg *(Figure 174)*	Tighten screws
8.	Nut or fill ring on top of tuning peg is loose *(Figure 175)*	Tighten the nut
9.	Screw that holds tuner peg in place is loose *(Figure 176)*	Tighten screw
10.	Loose string ends touching peg head or something else	Cut off string ends
11.	Worn out saddle	File top of saddle or replace saddle
12.	Worn out nut	Replace nut
13.	Loose bridge pin	Press bridge pin deeper in bridgepin hole
14.	Loose brace(s) and/or bridge plate (glued under the top on inside)	See professional repairman
15.	Loose saddle	Replace saddle
16.	Loose nut	Reglue nut
17.	Loose nut on adjustable trussrod	Tighten nut

Figure 174

Figure 175

Figure 176